Lucky Bright

PLANTS: Trees Coloring book Large print easy pages

Copyright © 2022 Lucky Bright

All rights reserved.
No part of this colorbook may be reproduced, or stored in a retrieval system, or transmitted in any form or by any means, electronic, mechanical, photocopying, recording, or otherwise, without express written permission of the publisher.

ISBN: 9798429719245

Trees

Nature is our wealth. This amazing and beautiful world surrounds a person. Looking around you can see what nature has created. Forests, rivers and lakes, fields and steppes, mountains and plains are unique in their own way.
The natural world is very rich and varied. There are hundreds of thousands of tree species, many of which we have never seen in our lives.
It is time to start getting curious about trees.
This is a great time to coloring book. Easy pictures of trees are perfect for relaxing and stress-relieving for adults and seniors. It's also easy for kids who are just learning to color.

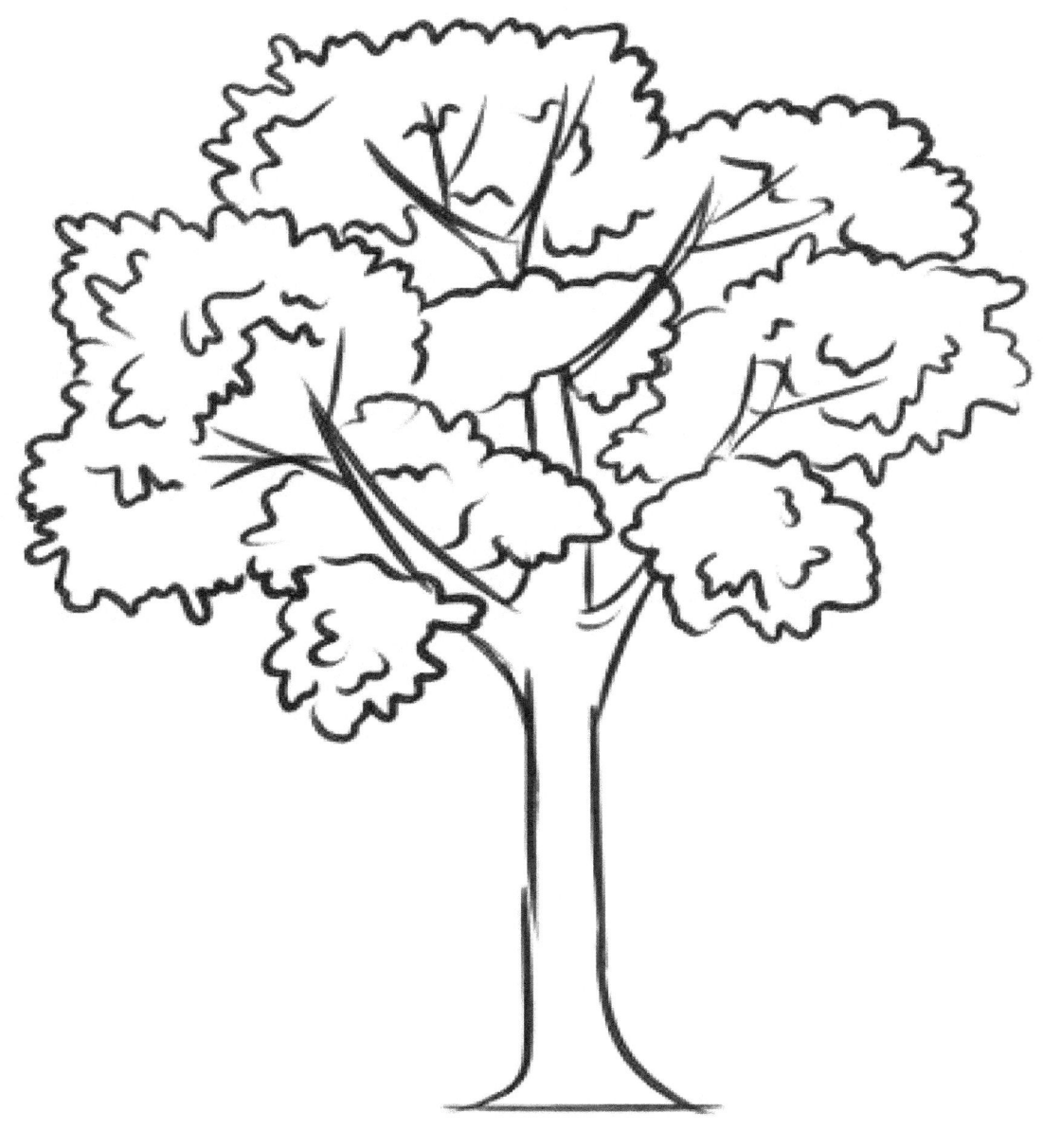

Ash Tree

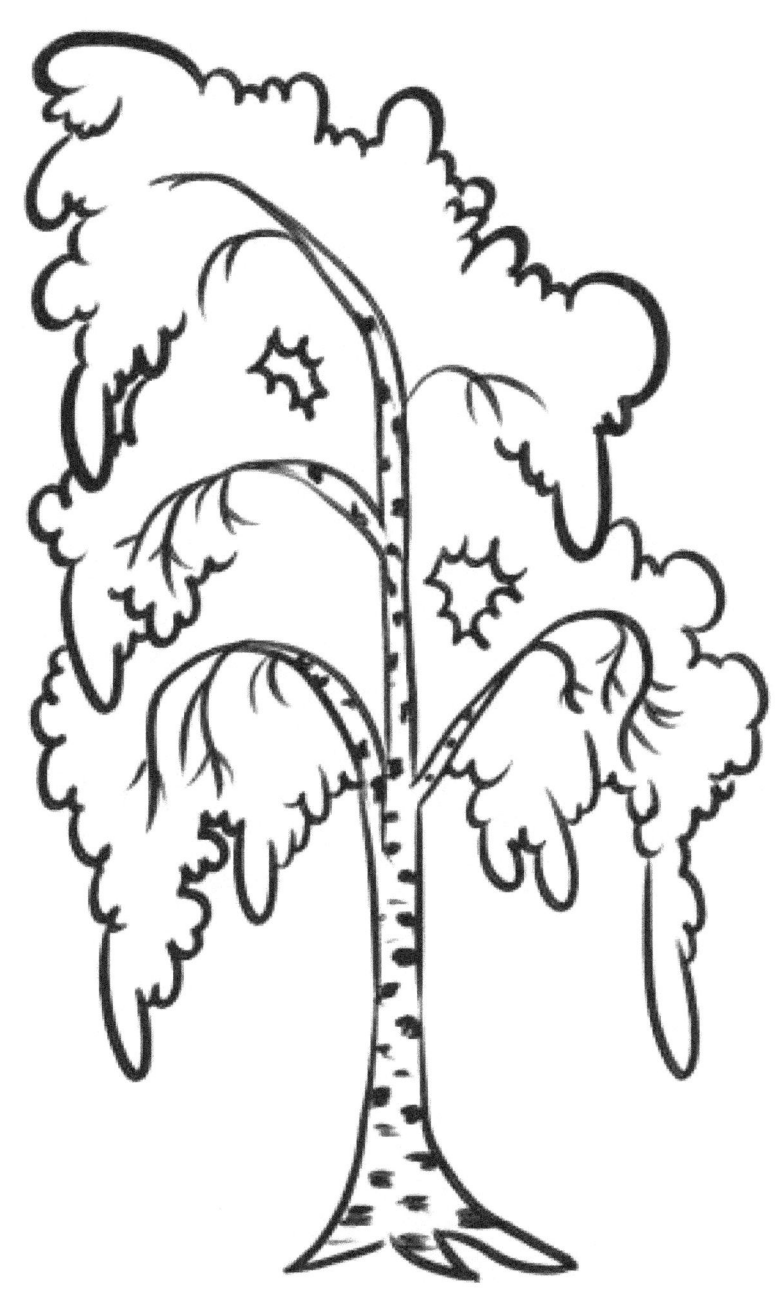

Birch Tree

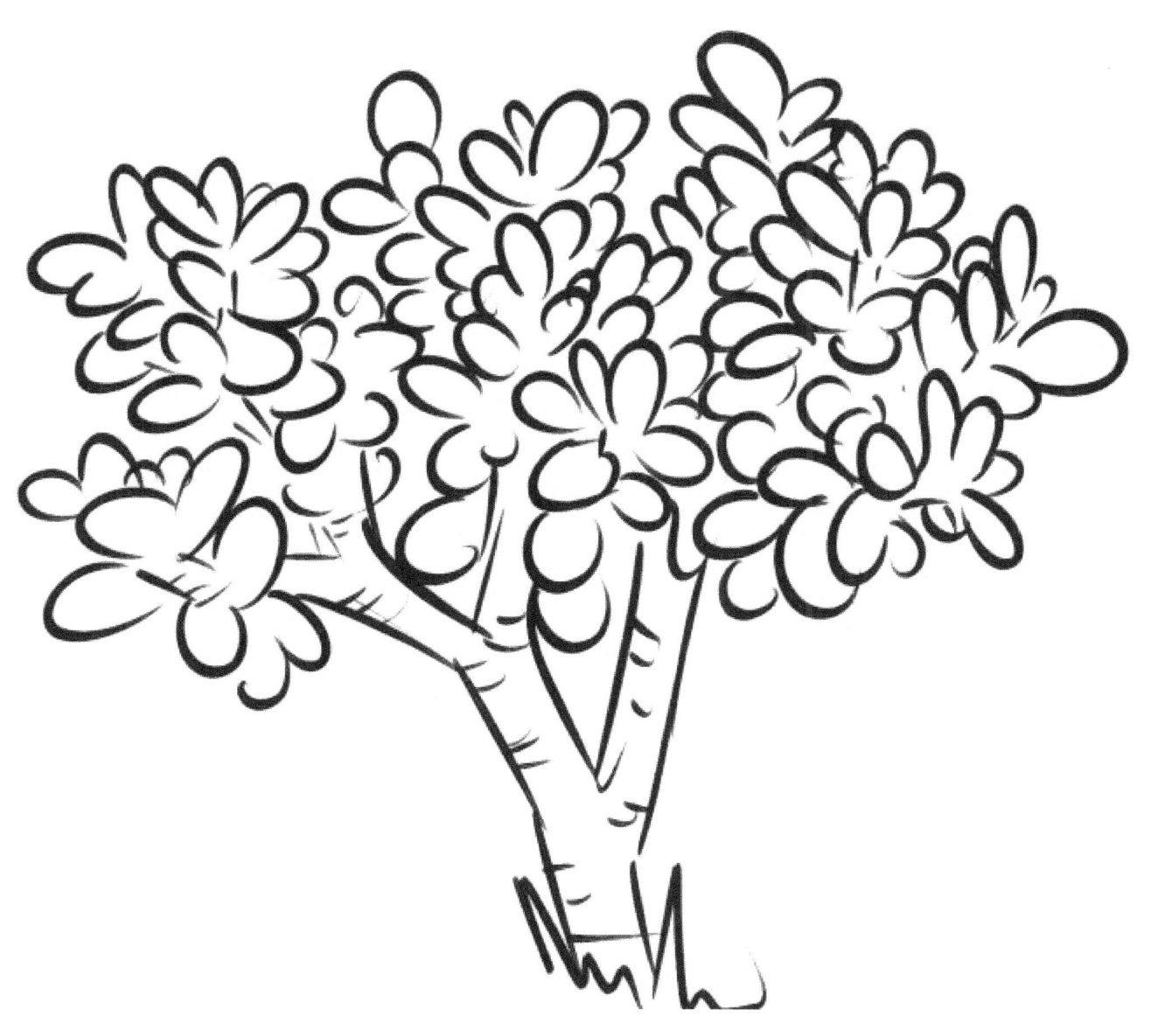

Jade Tree

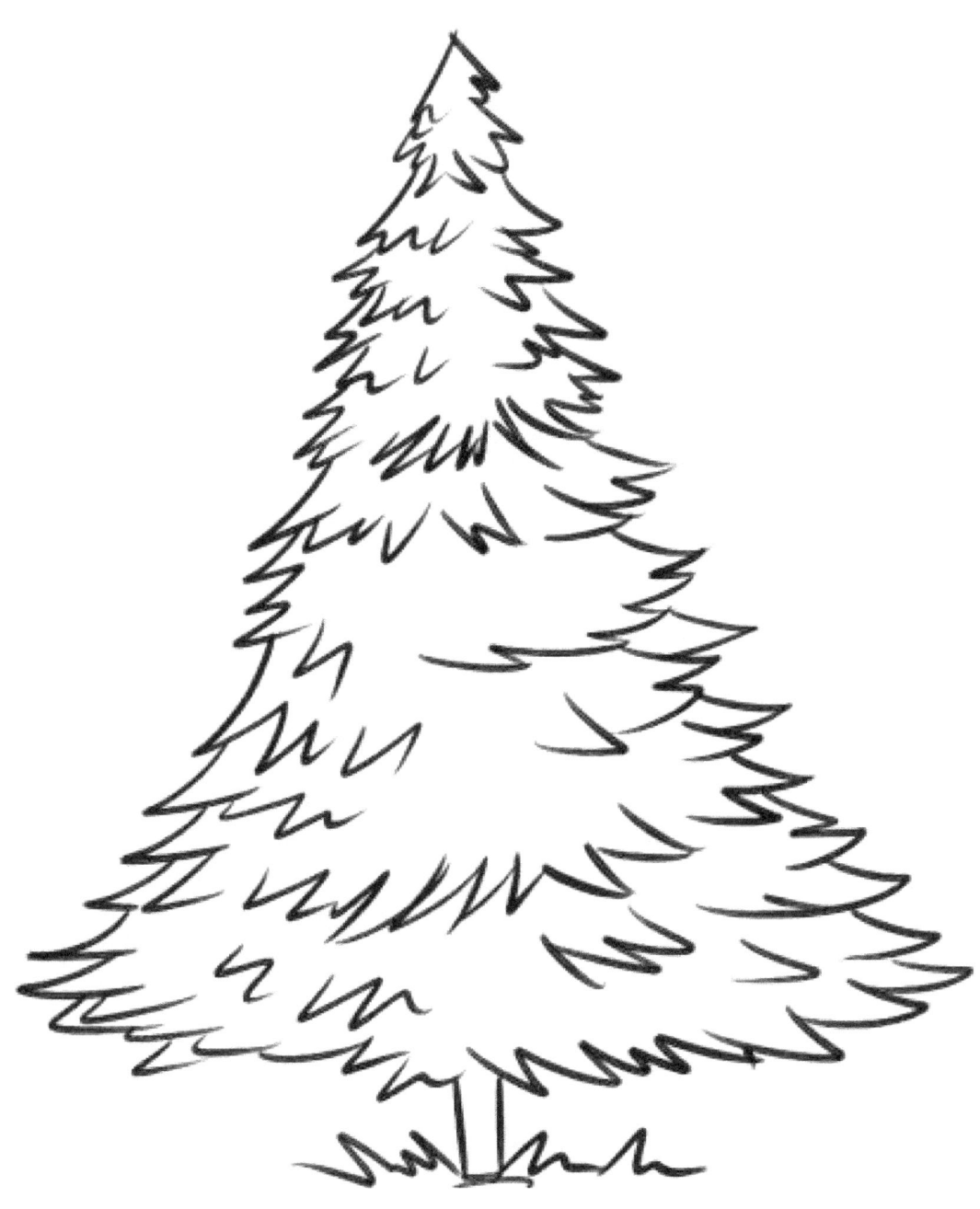

Fir Tree

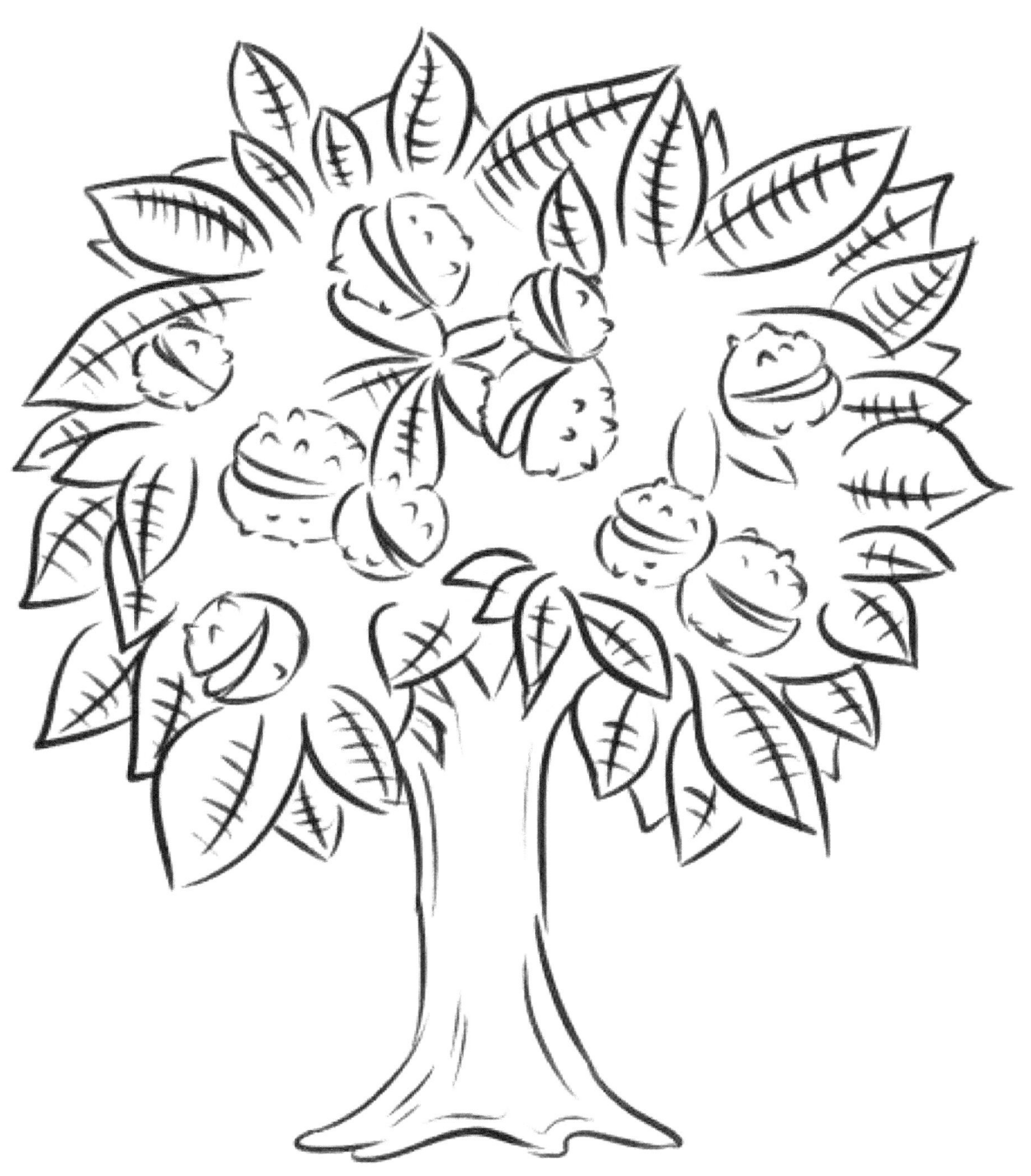

Chestnut Tree

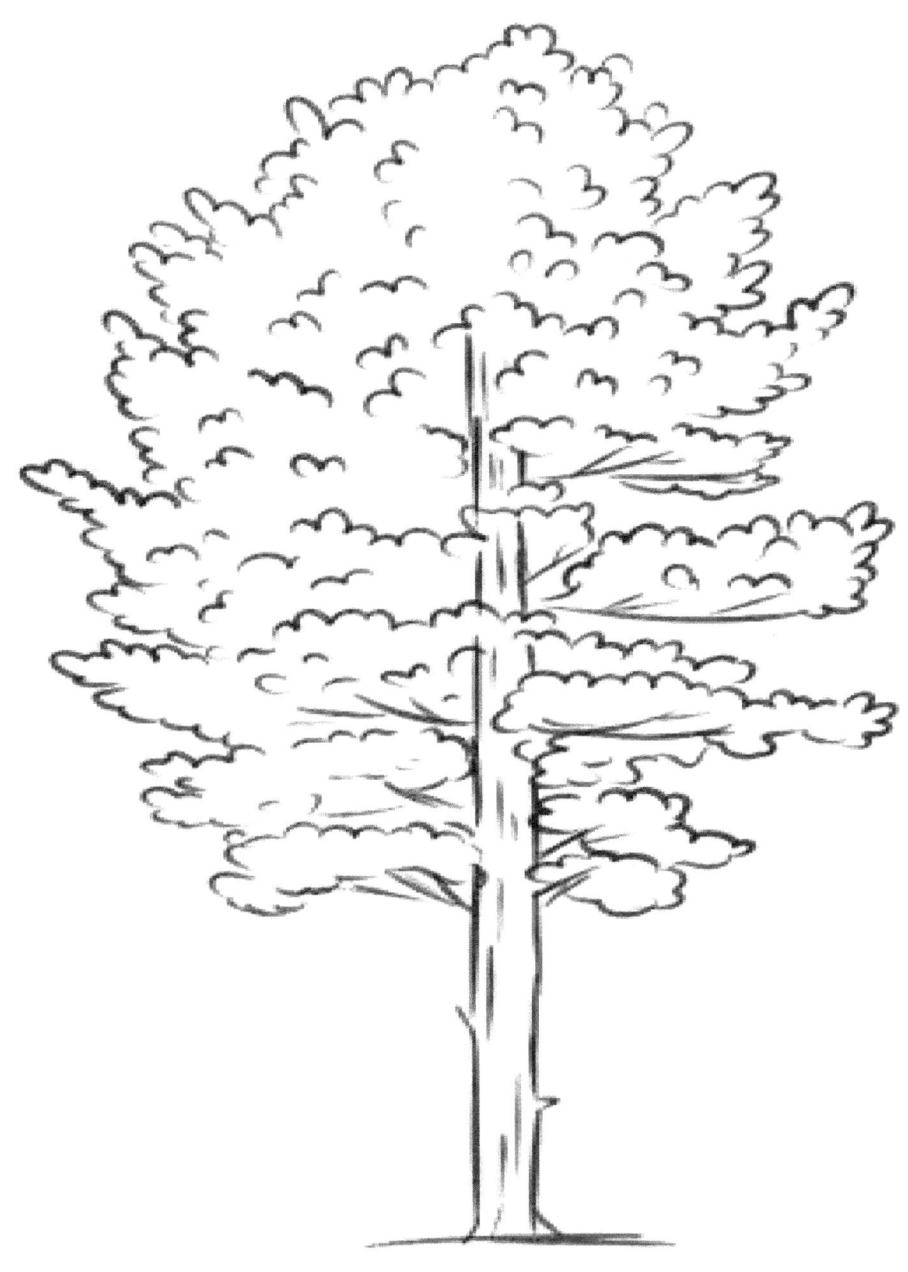

Cedar Tree

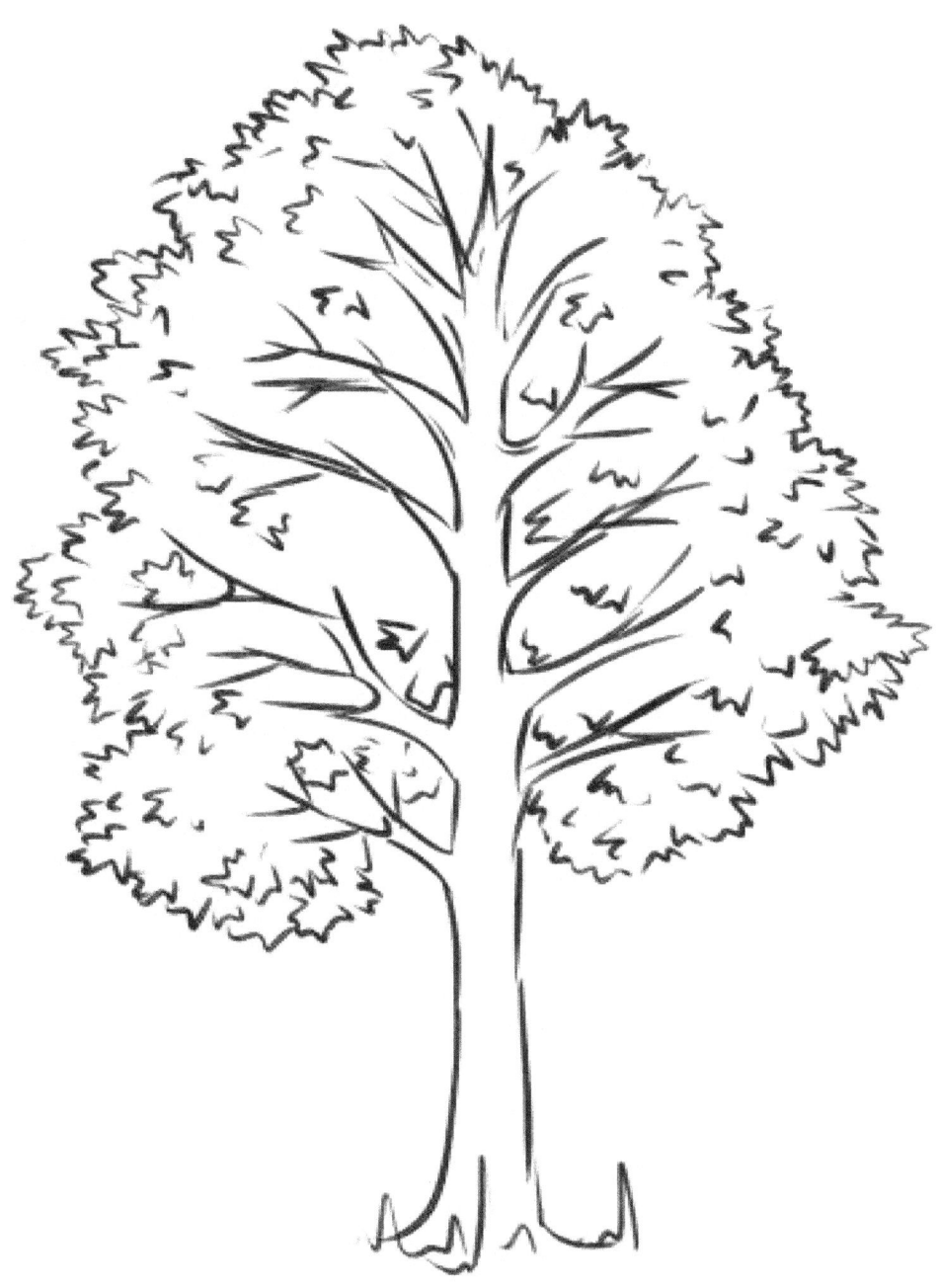

Maple Tree

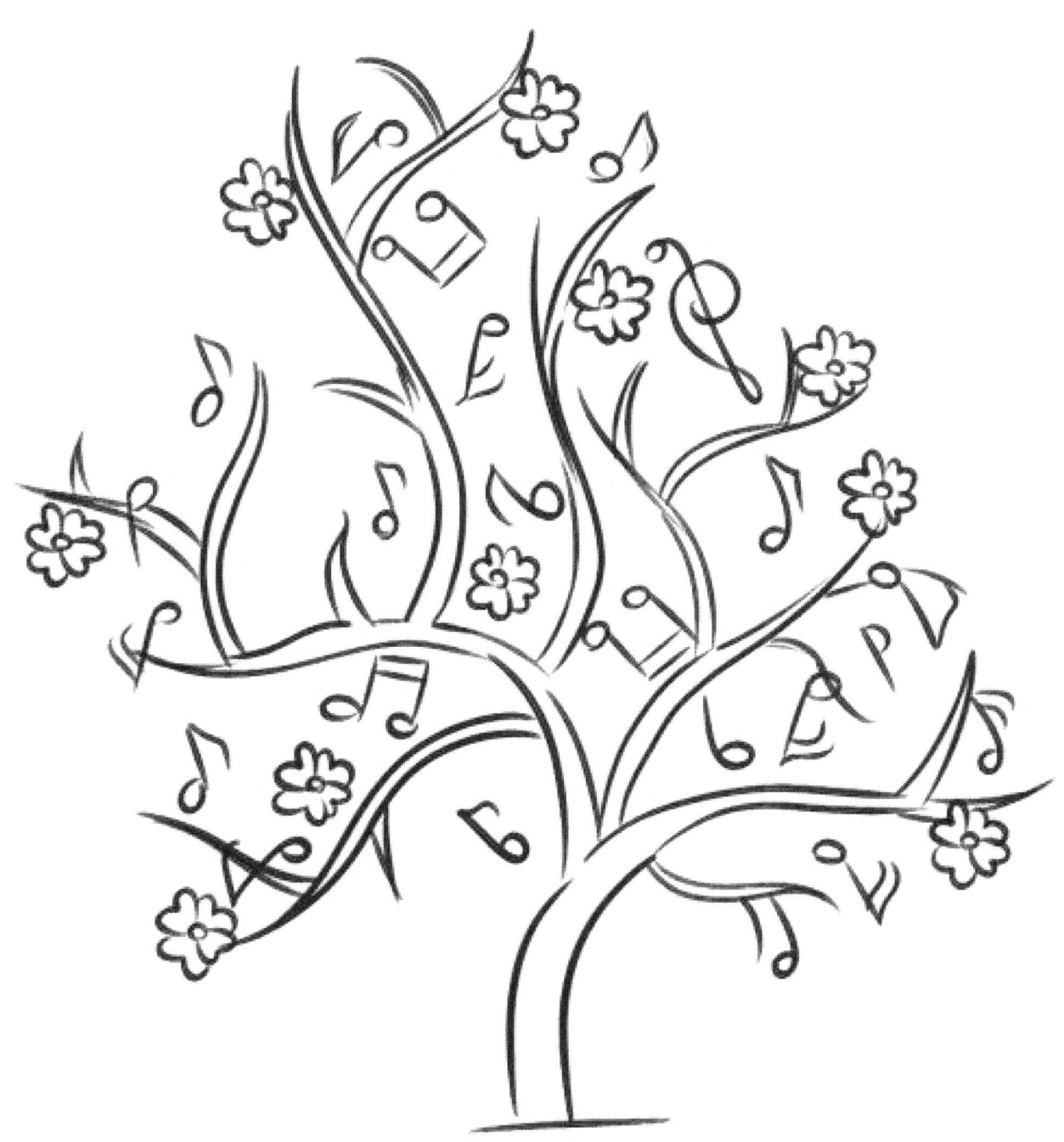

Music tree

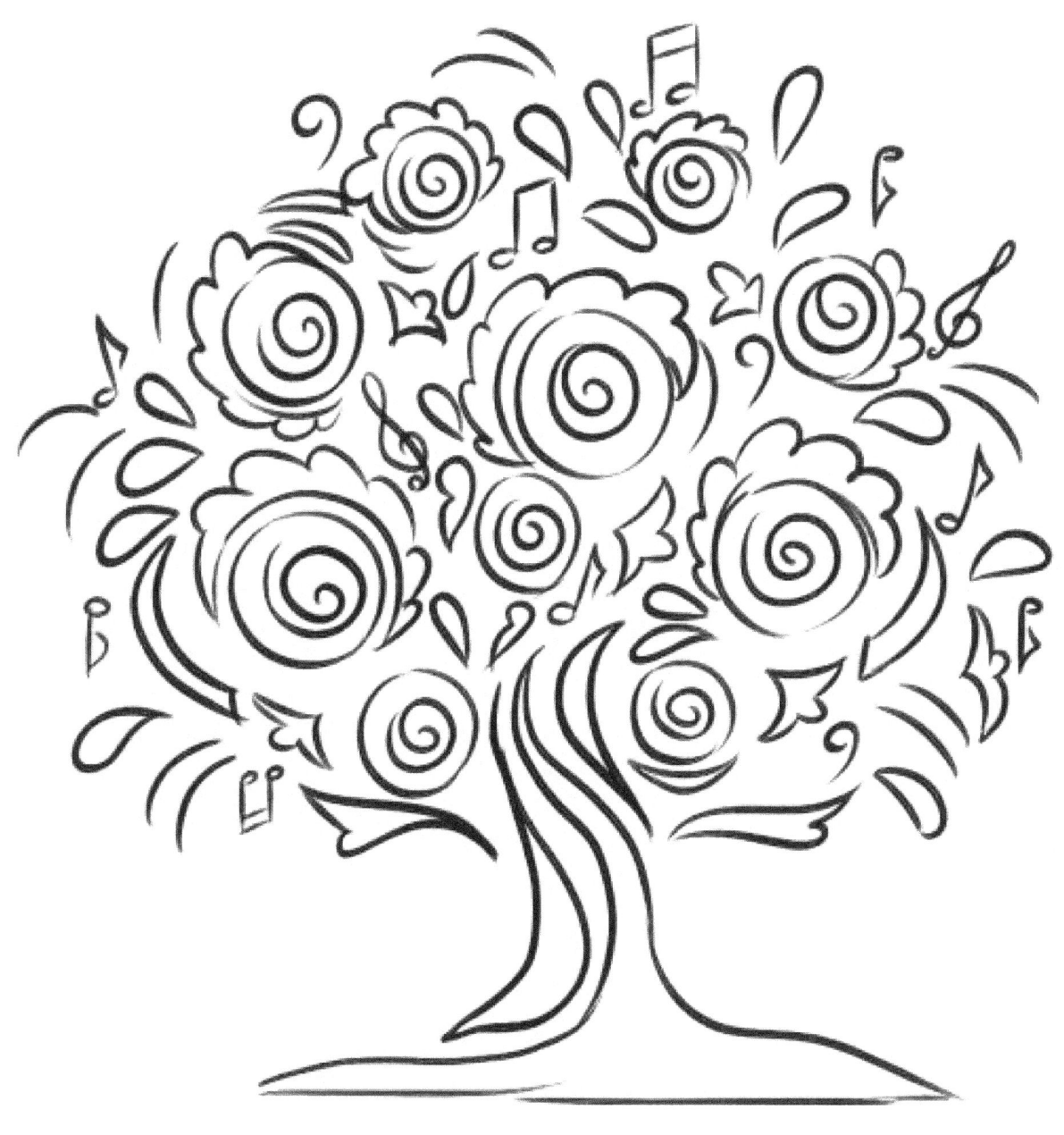

Music tree

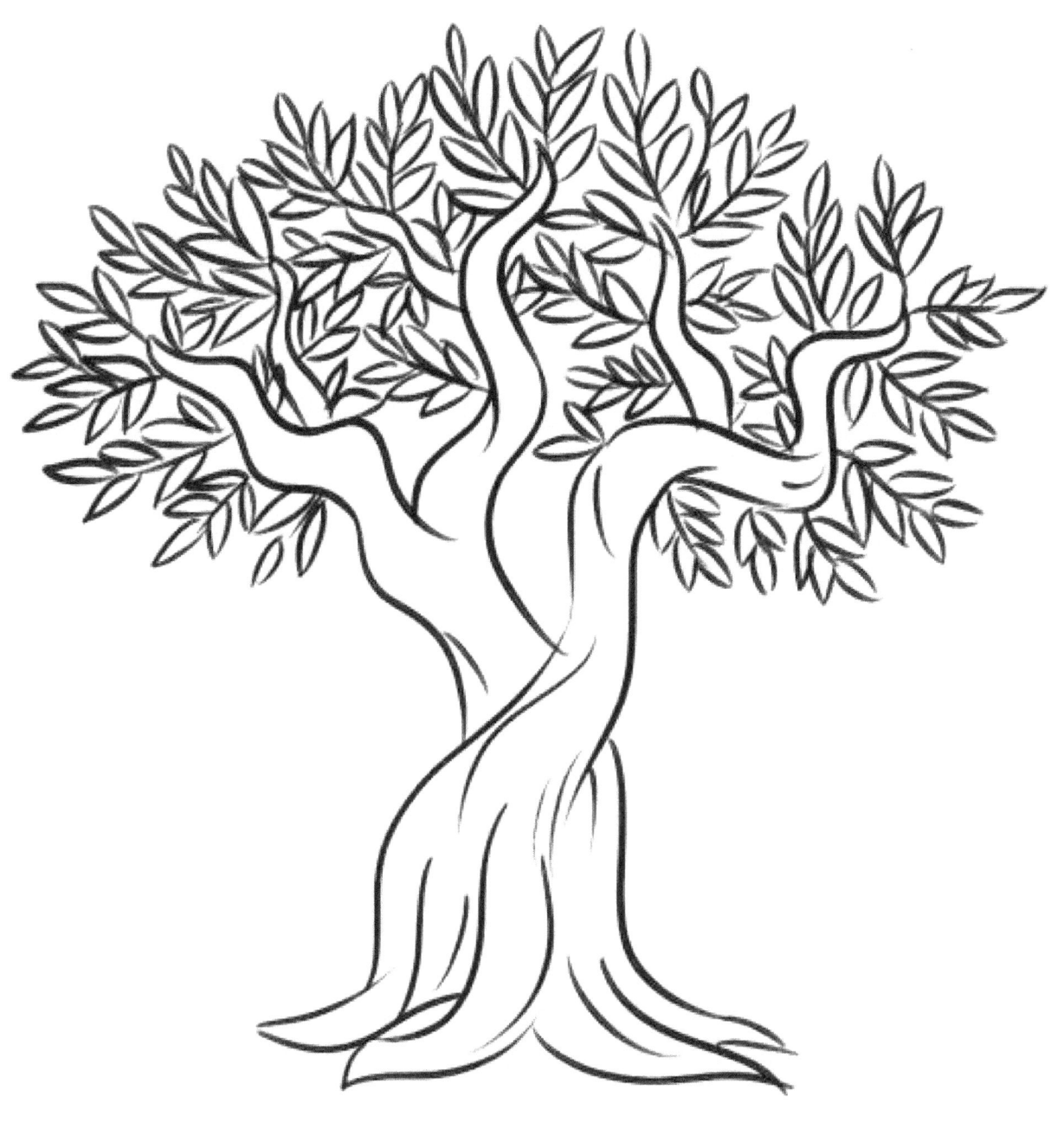

Olive Tree

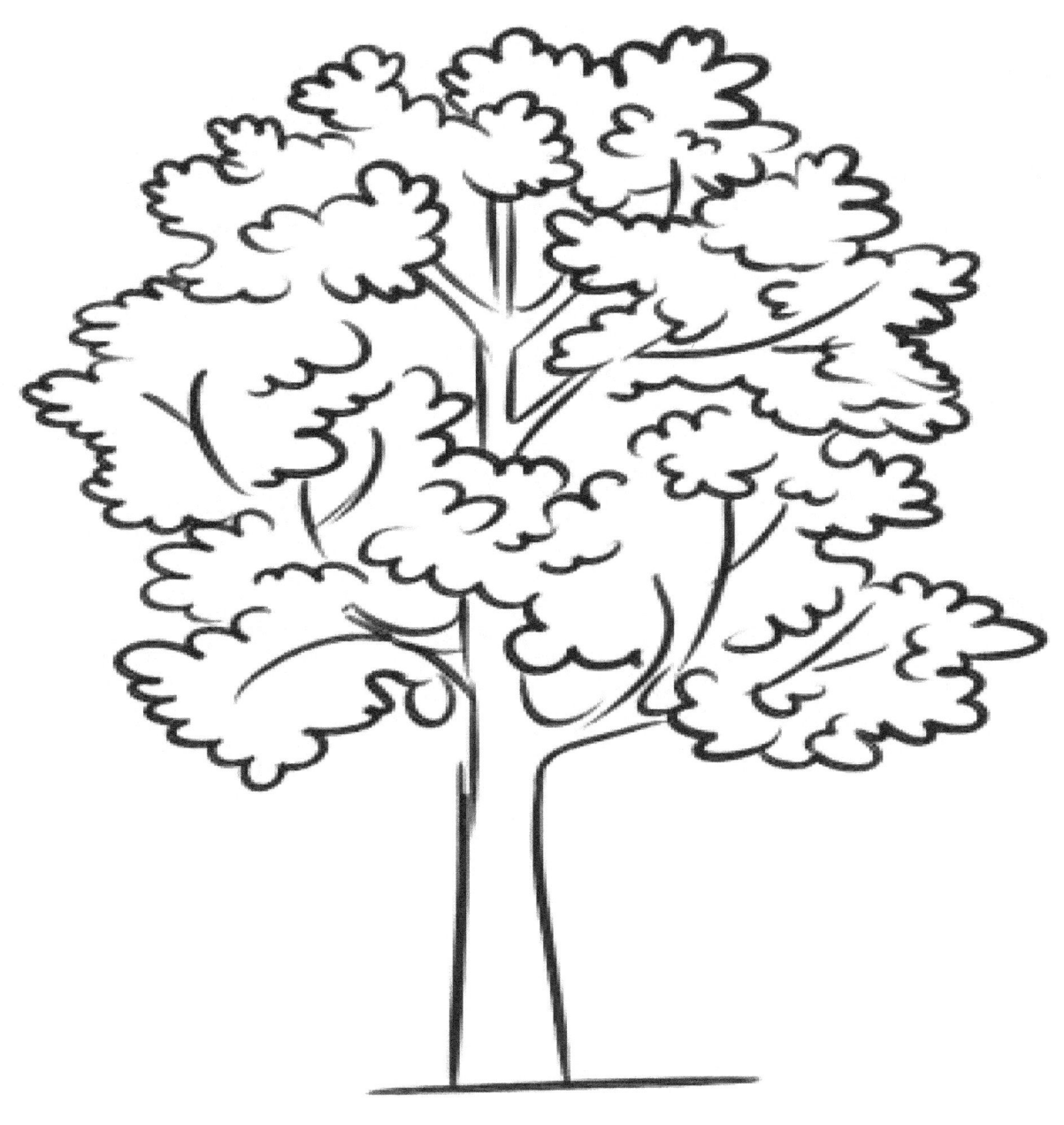

Aspen Tree

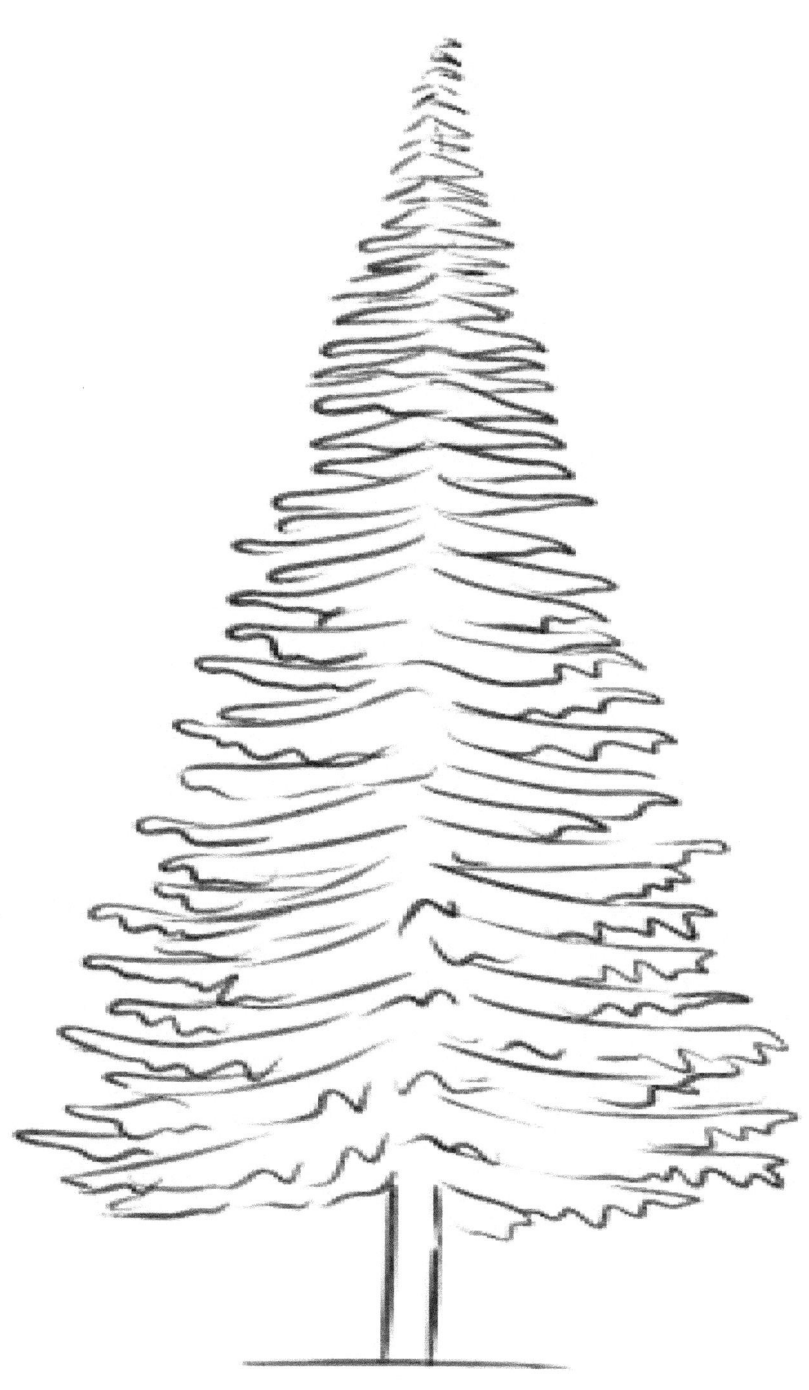

Fir Tree

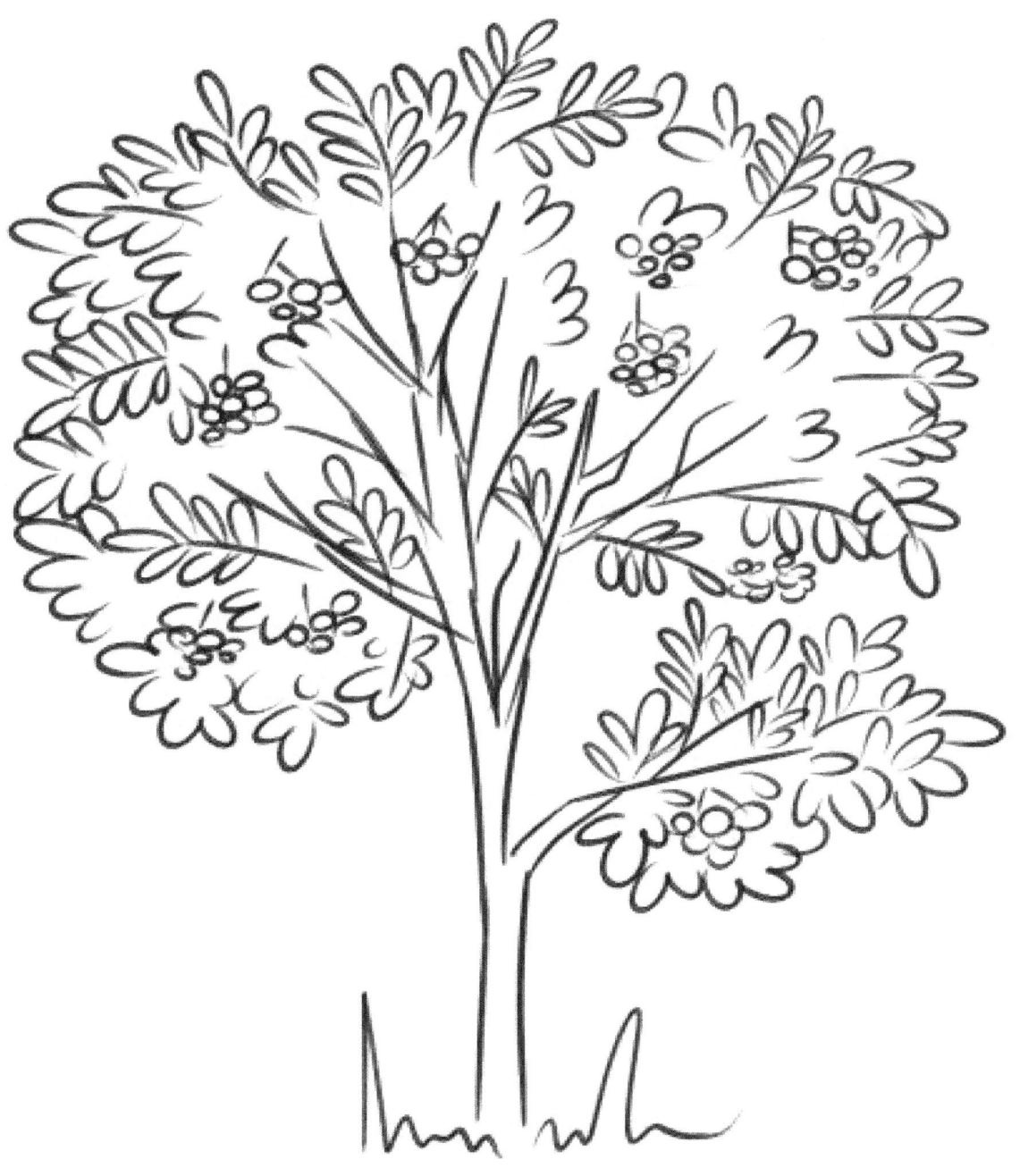

Ashberry Tree

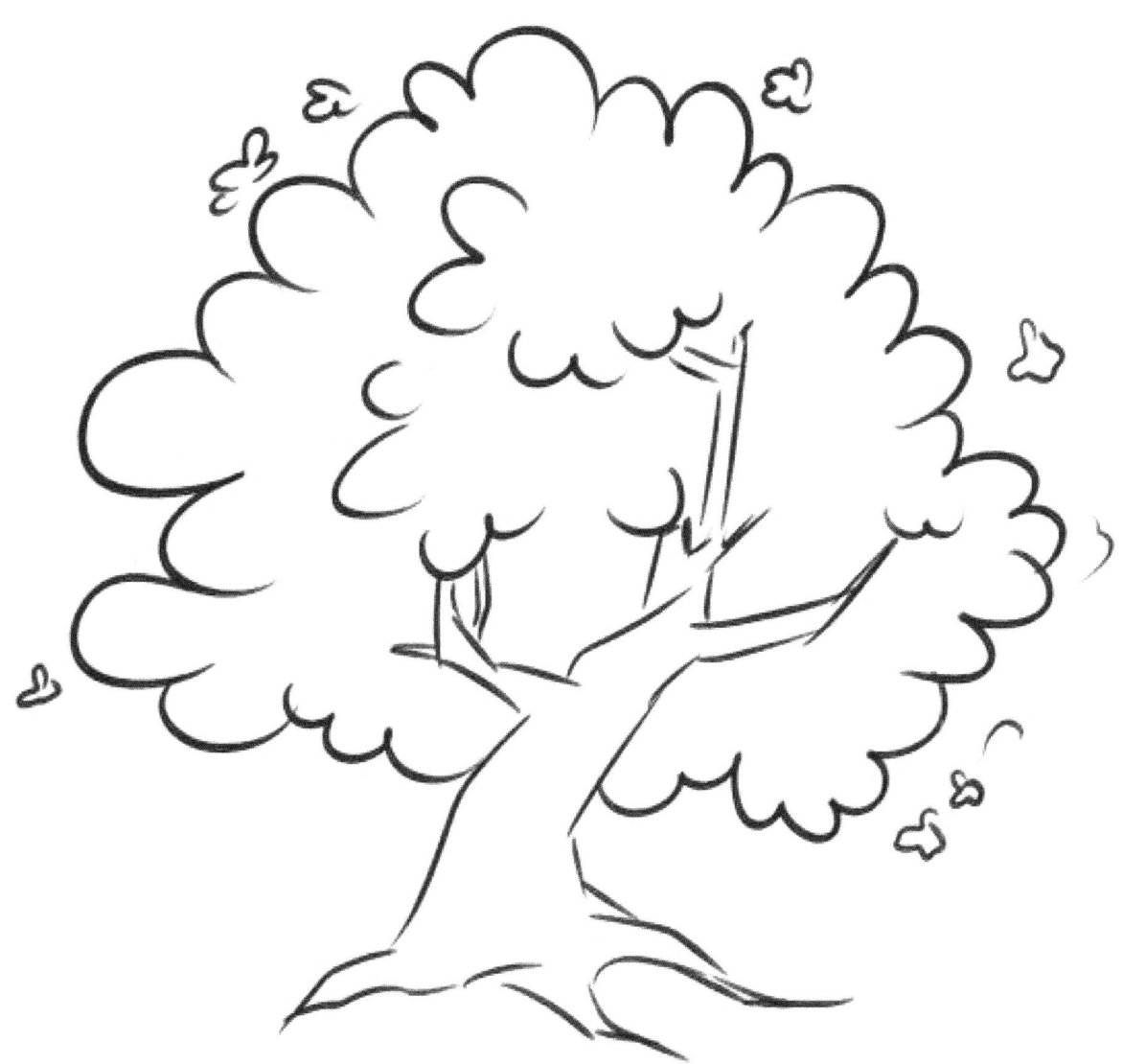

Sakura

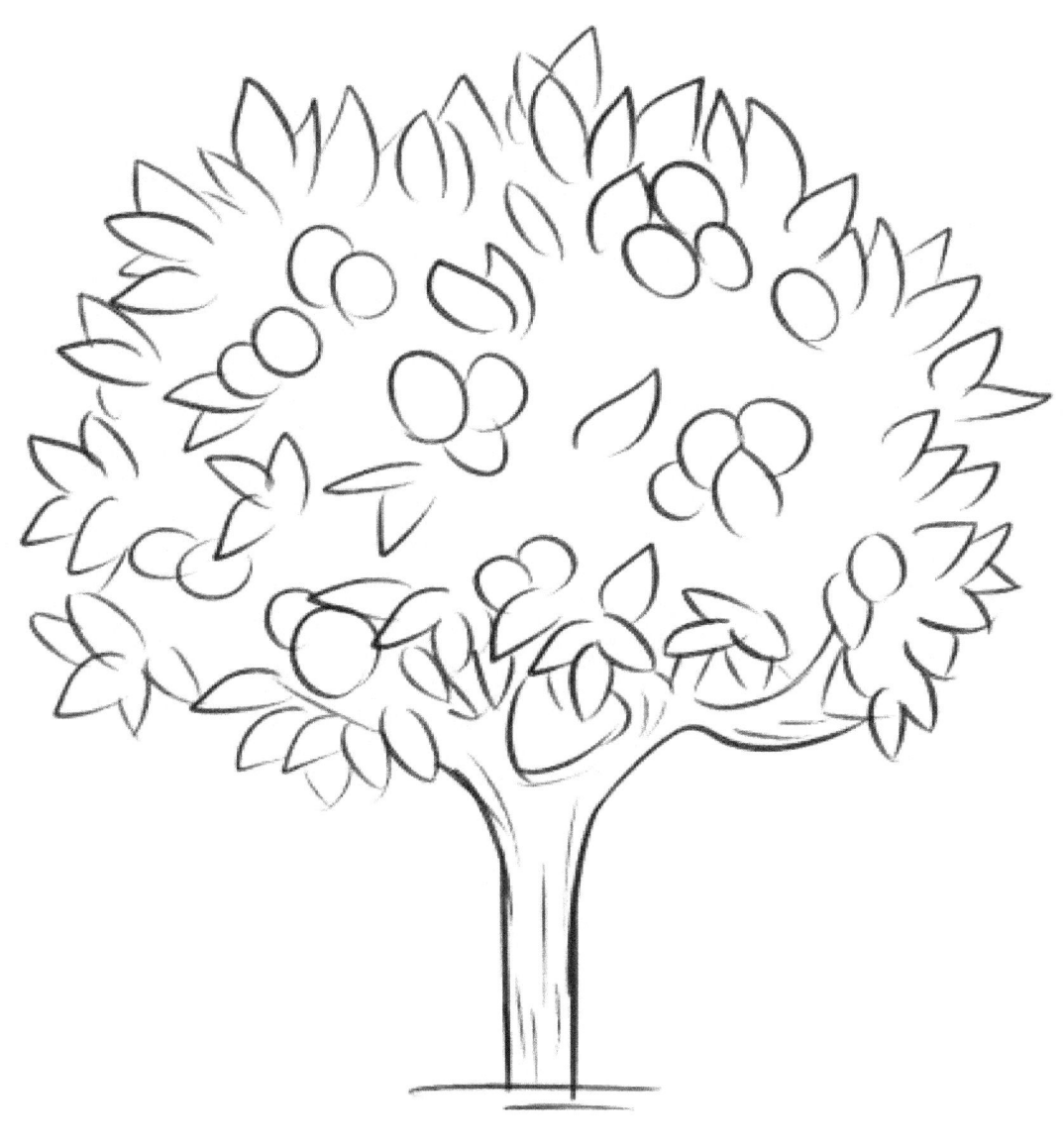

Plum Tree

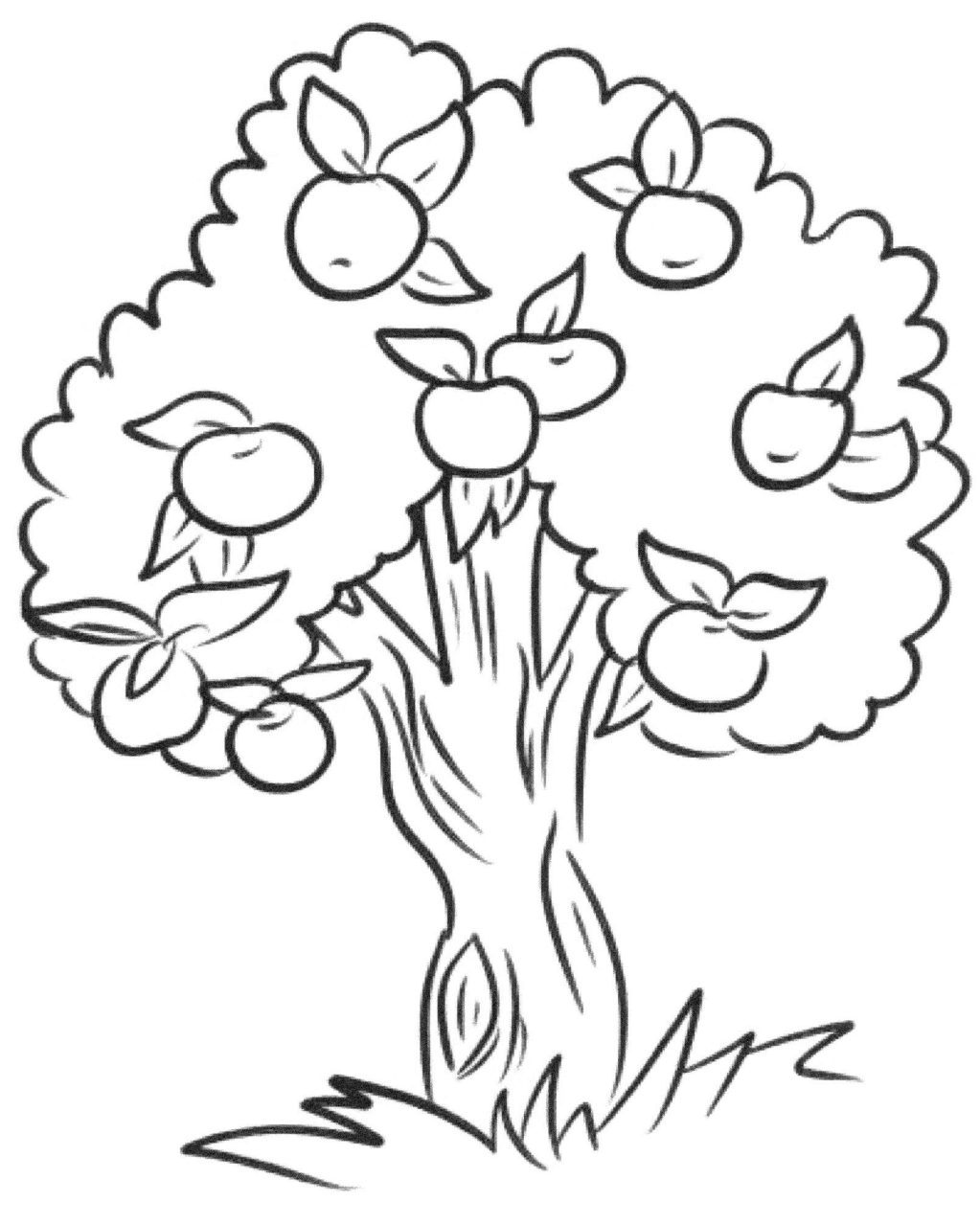

Apple Tree

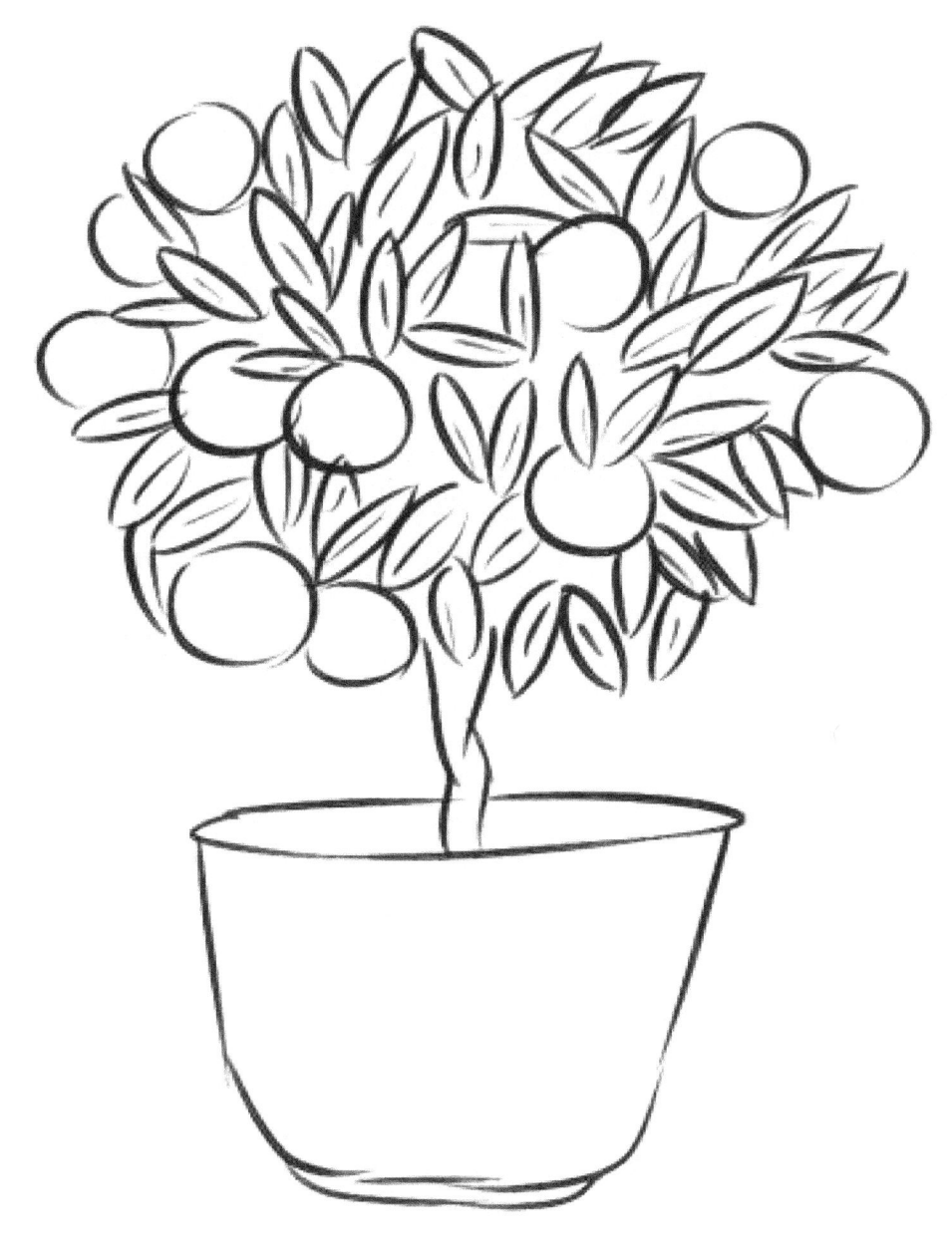

Apricot Tree in a pot

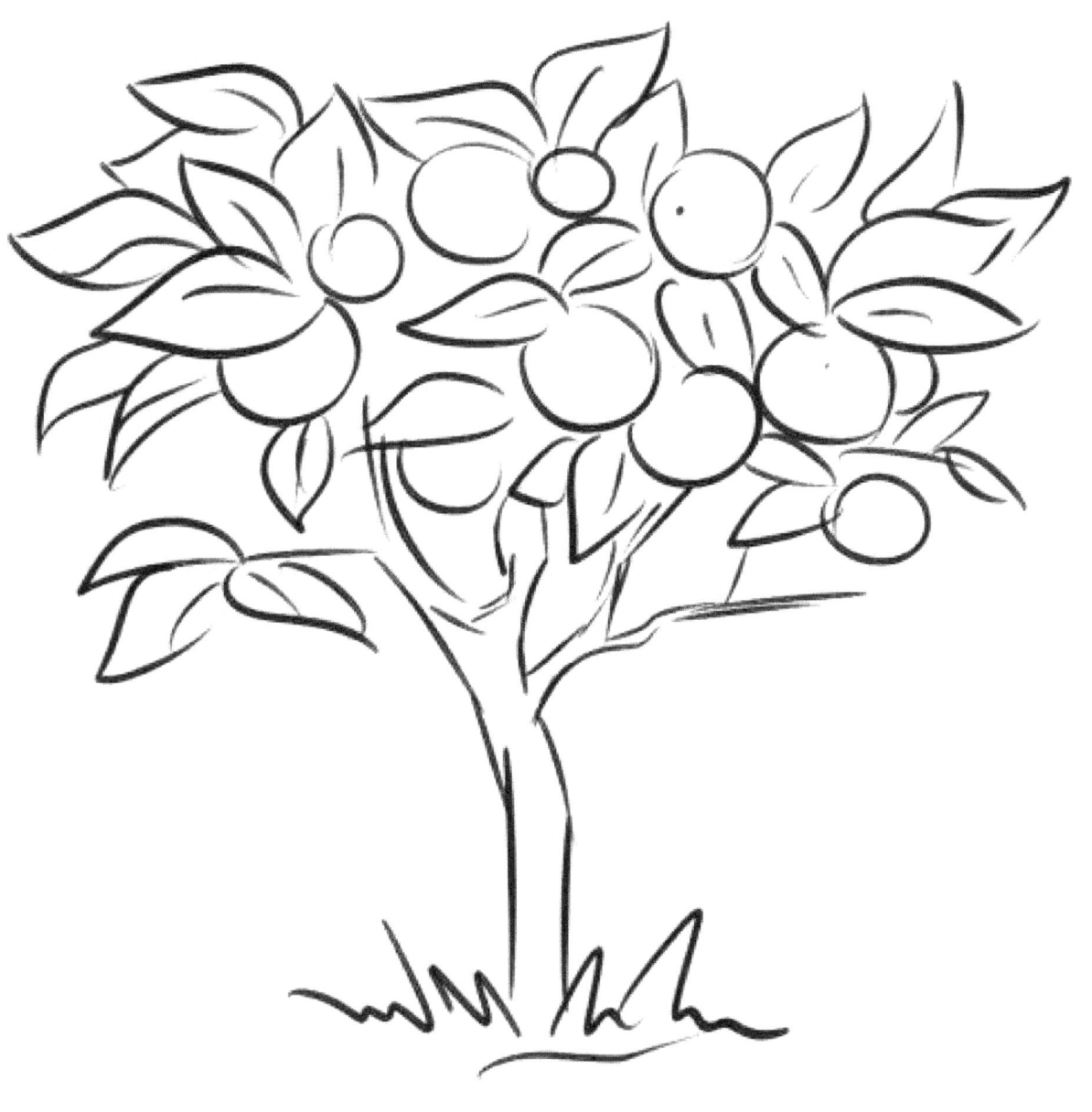

Orange Tree

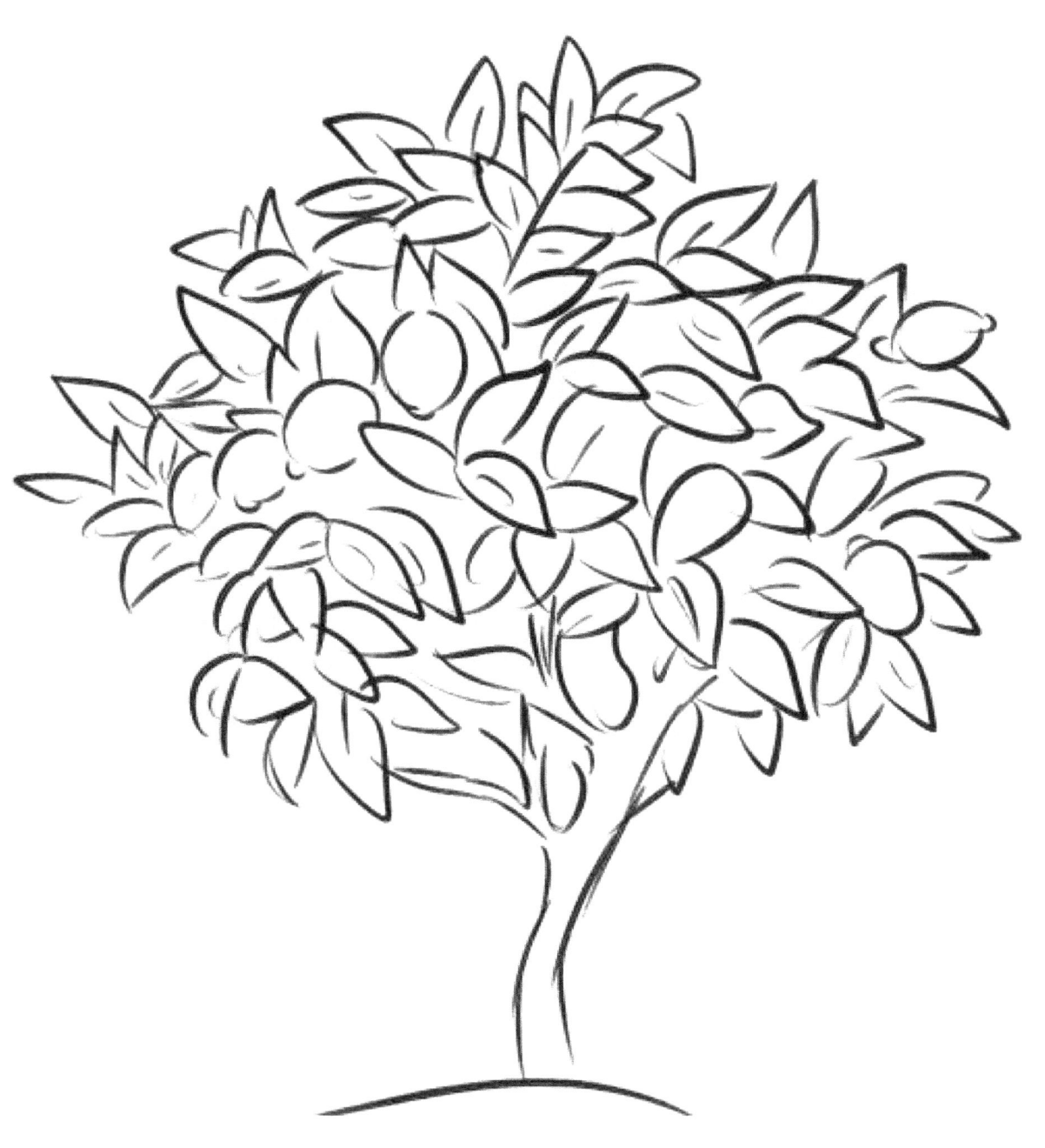

Lemon Tree

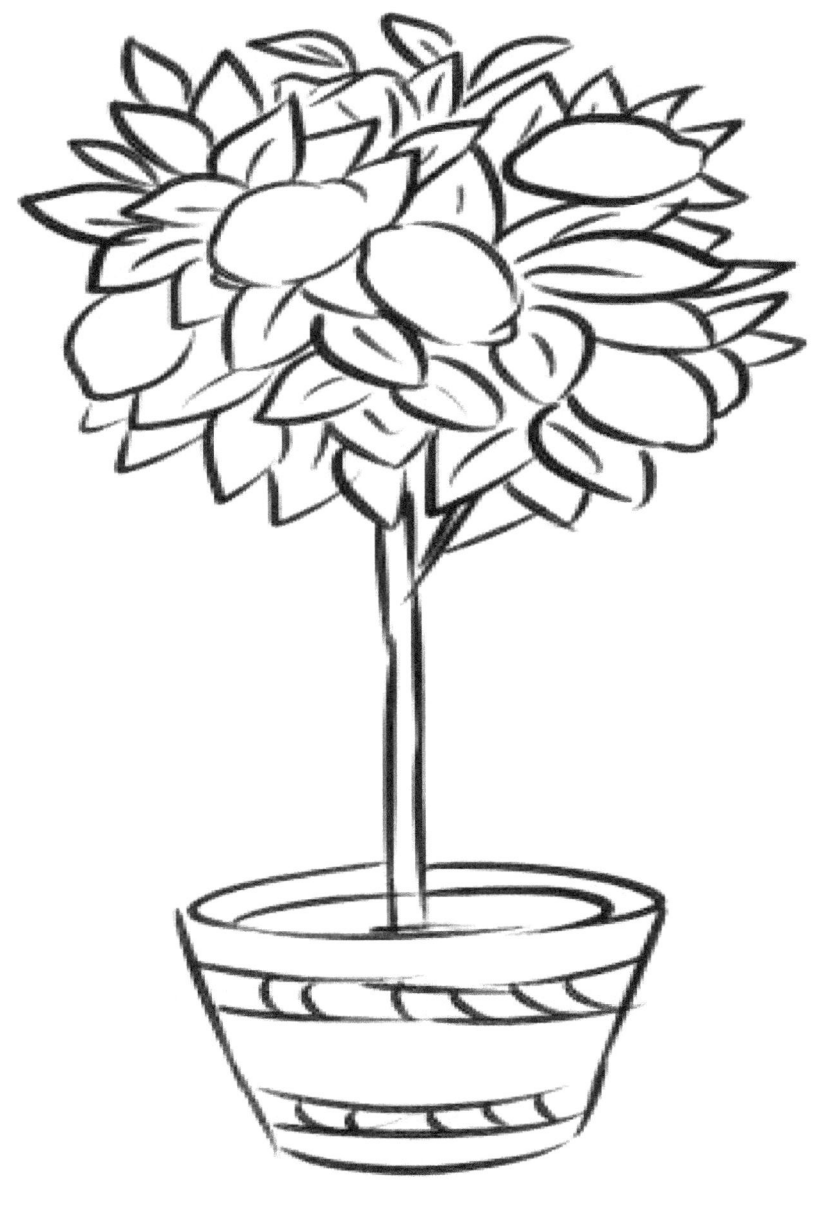

Lemon Tree in a pot

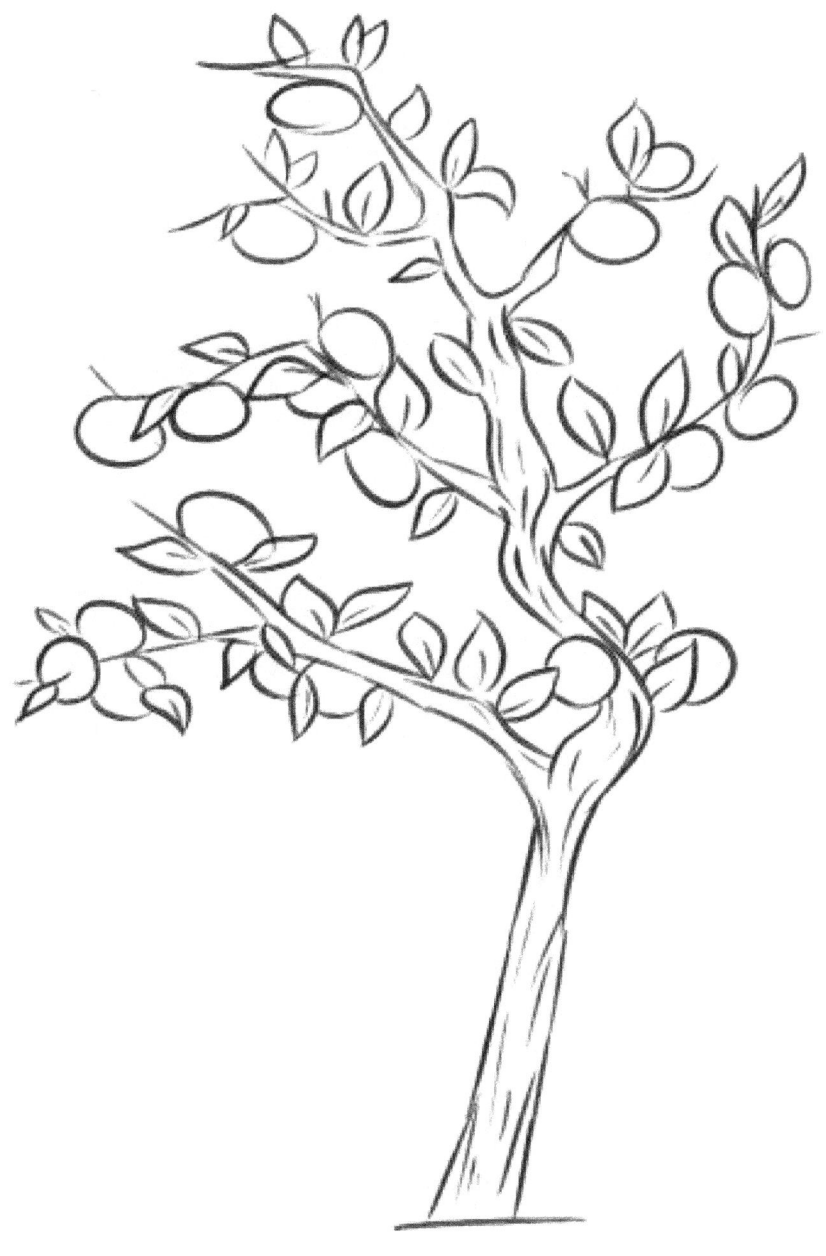

Tangerine Tree

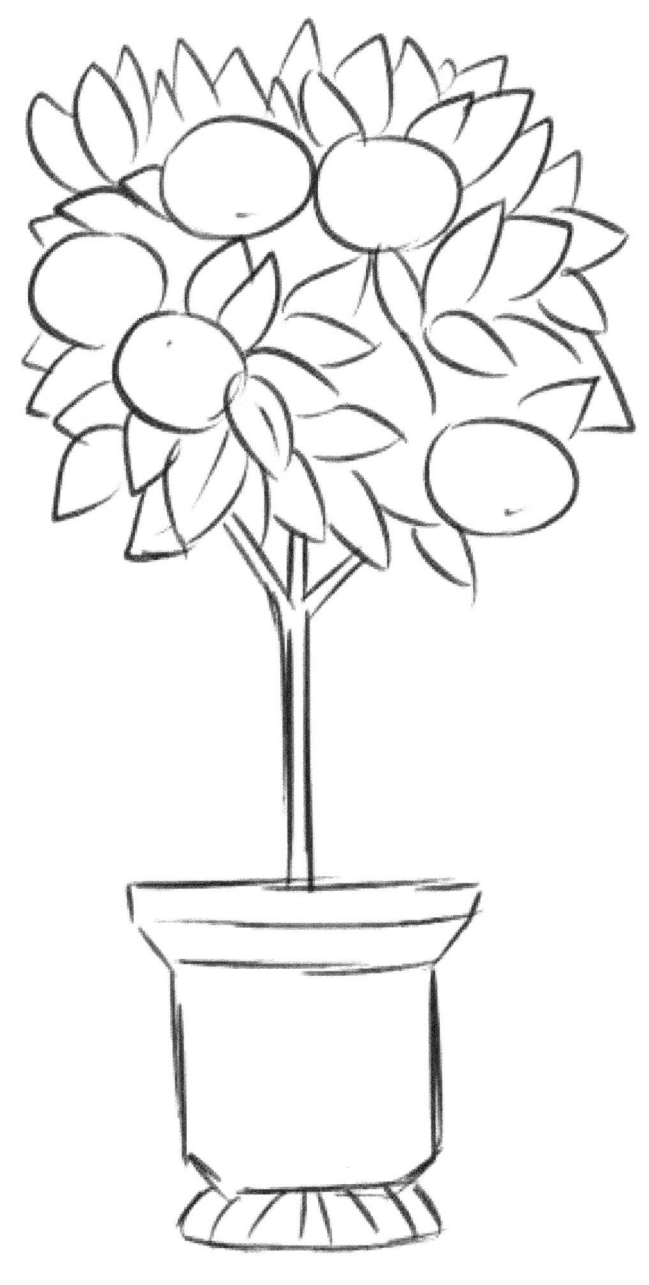

Tangerine tree in a pot

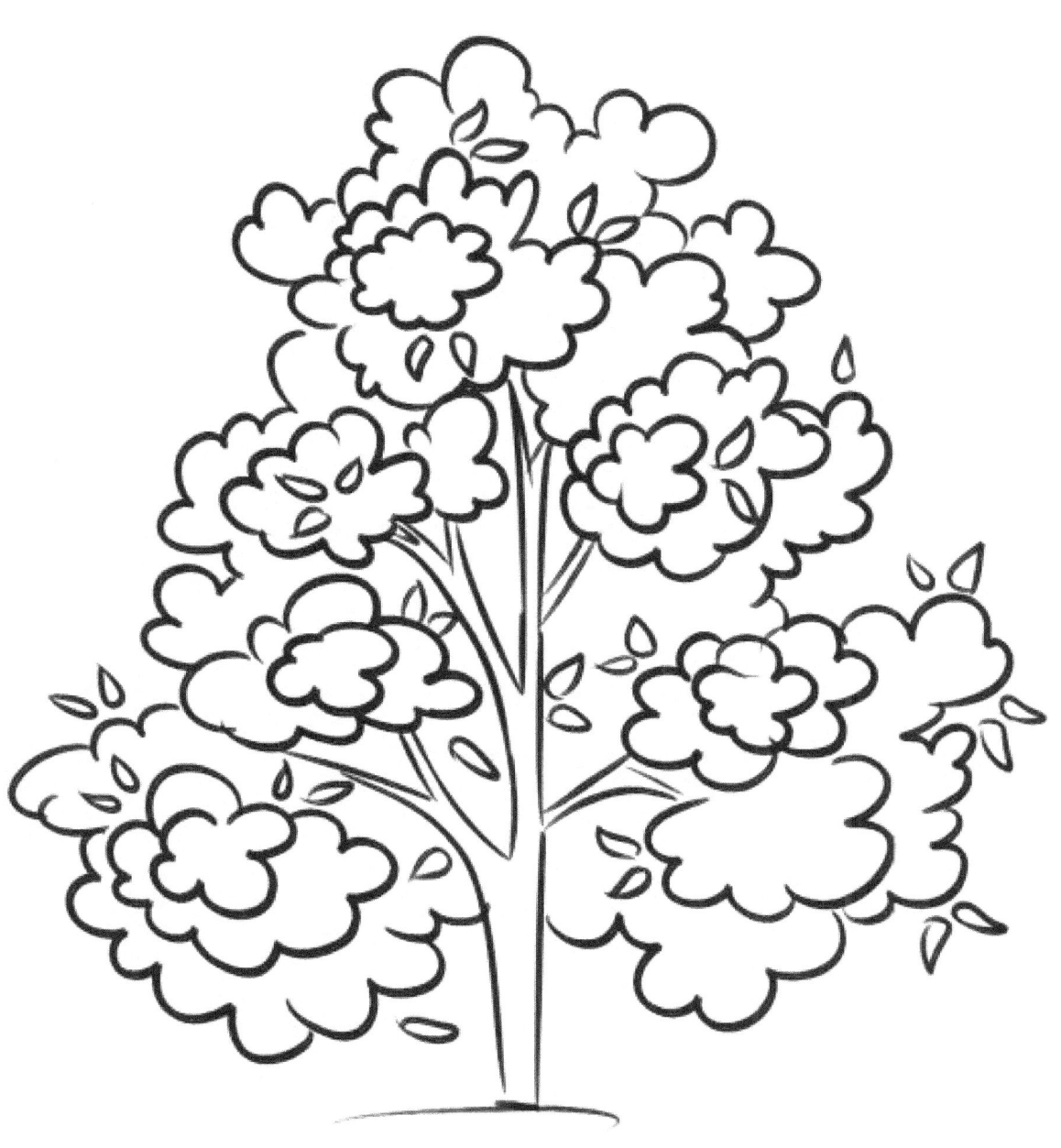

Fall tree

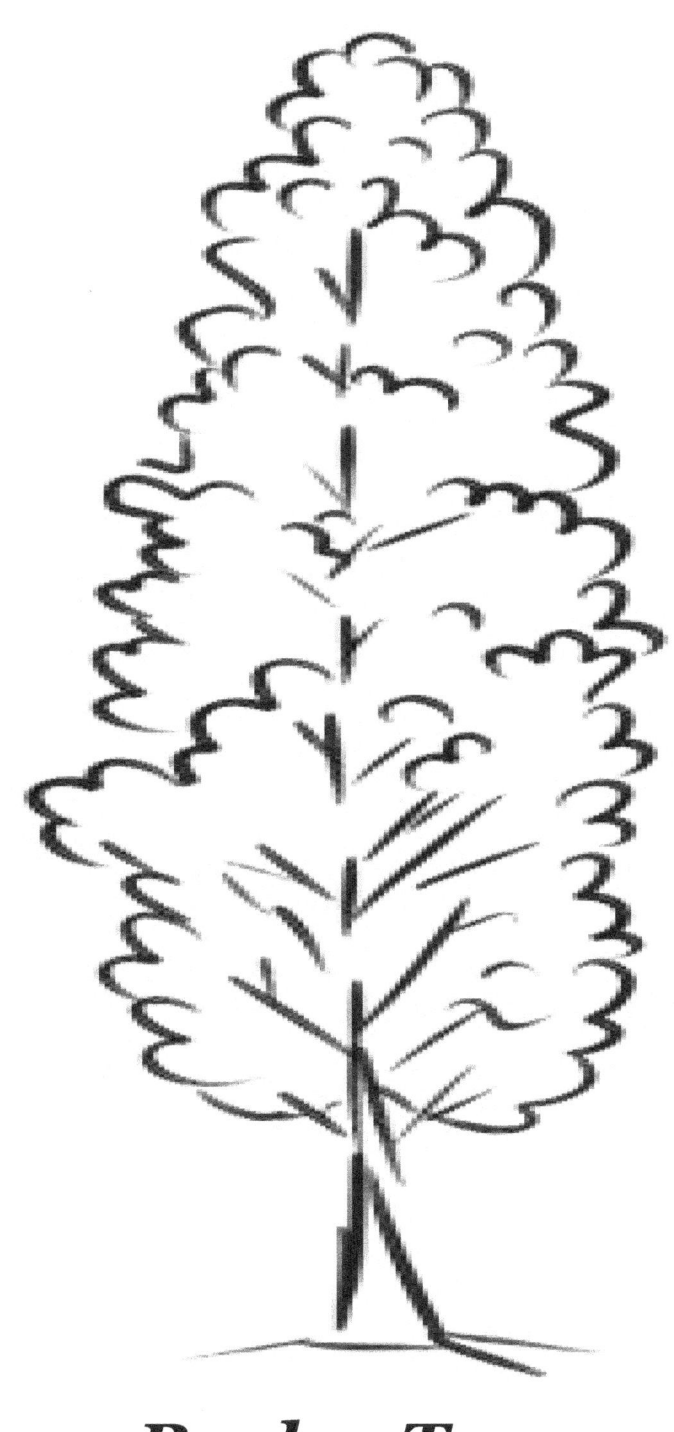

Poplar Tree

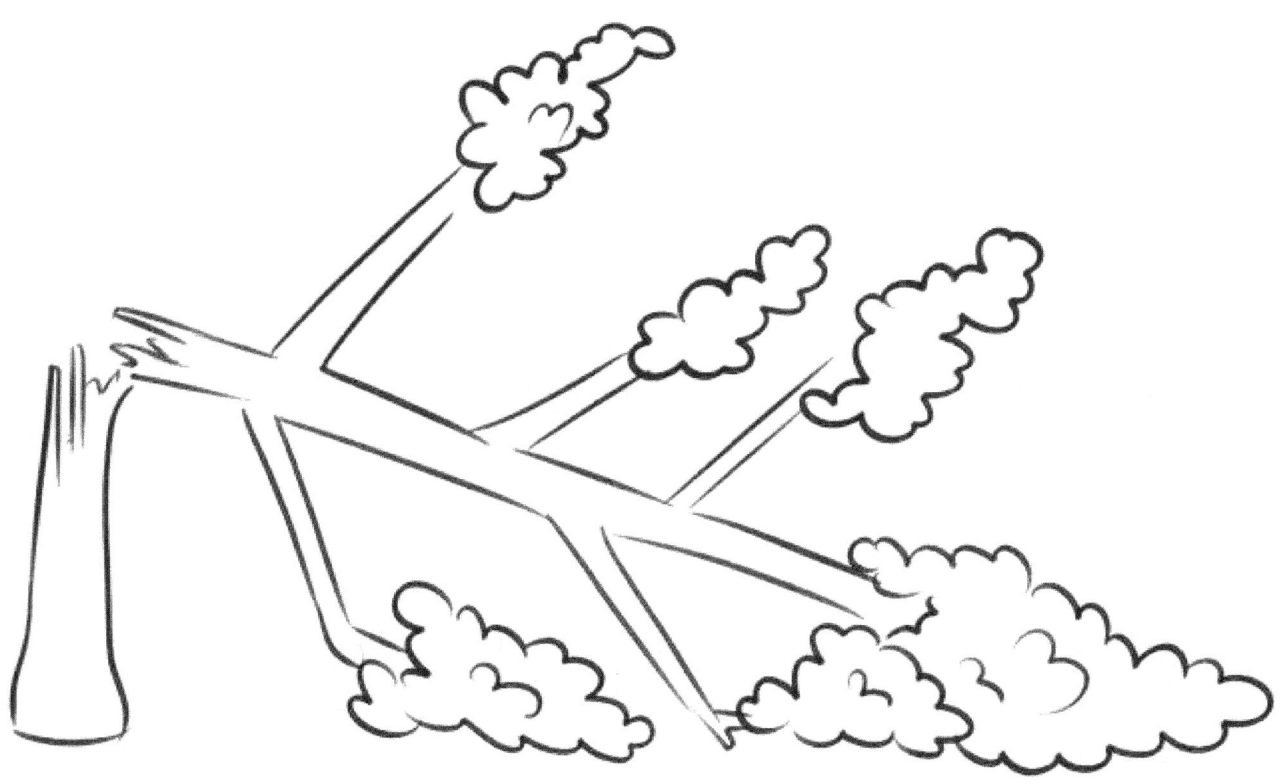

Broken tree

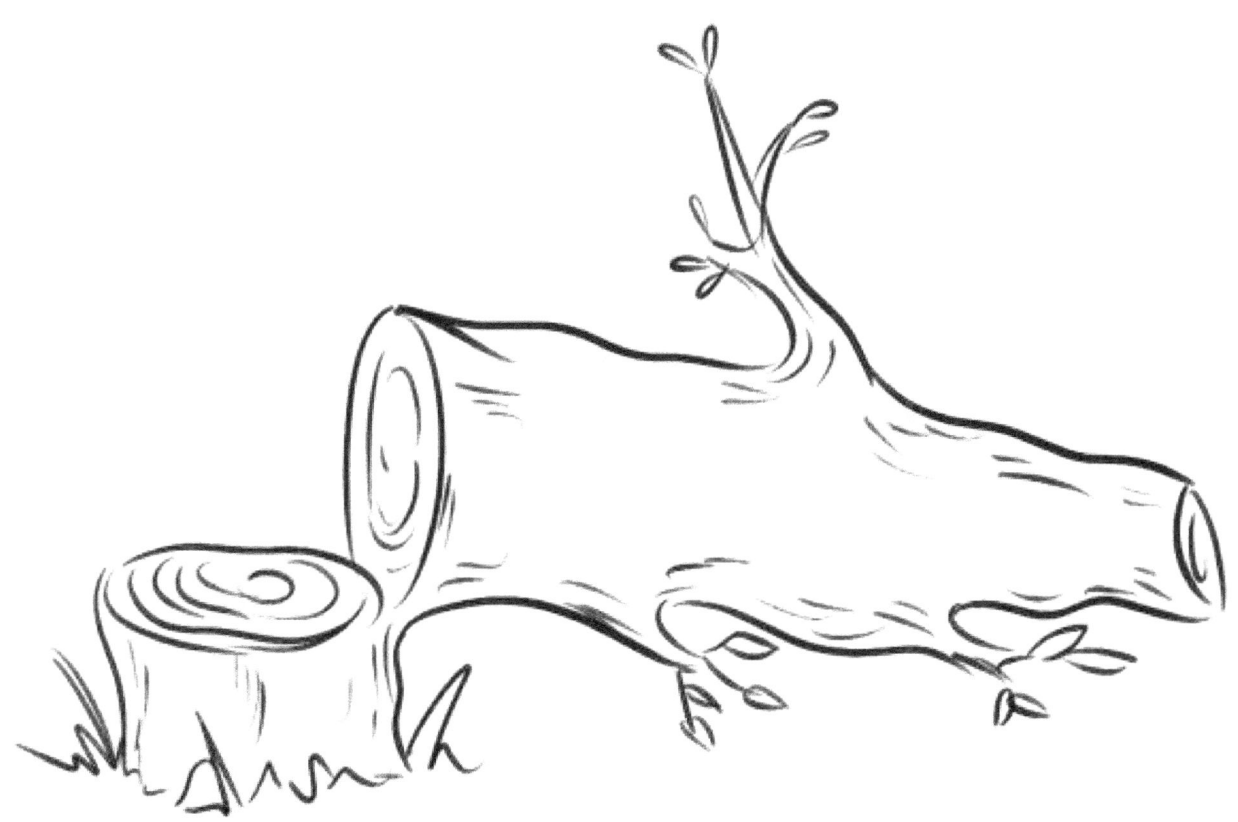

Cut down tree

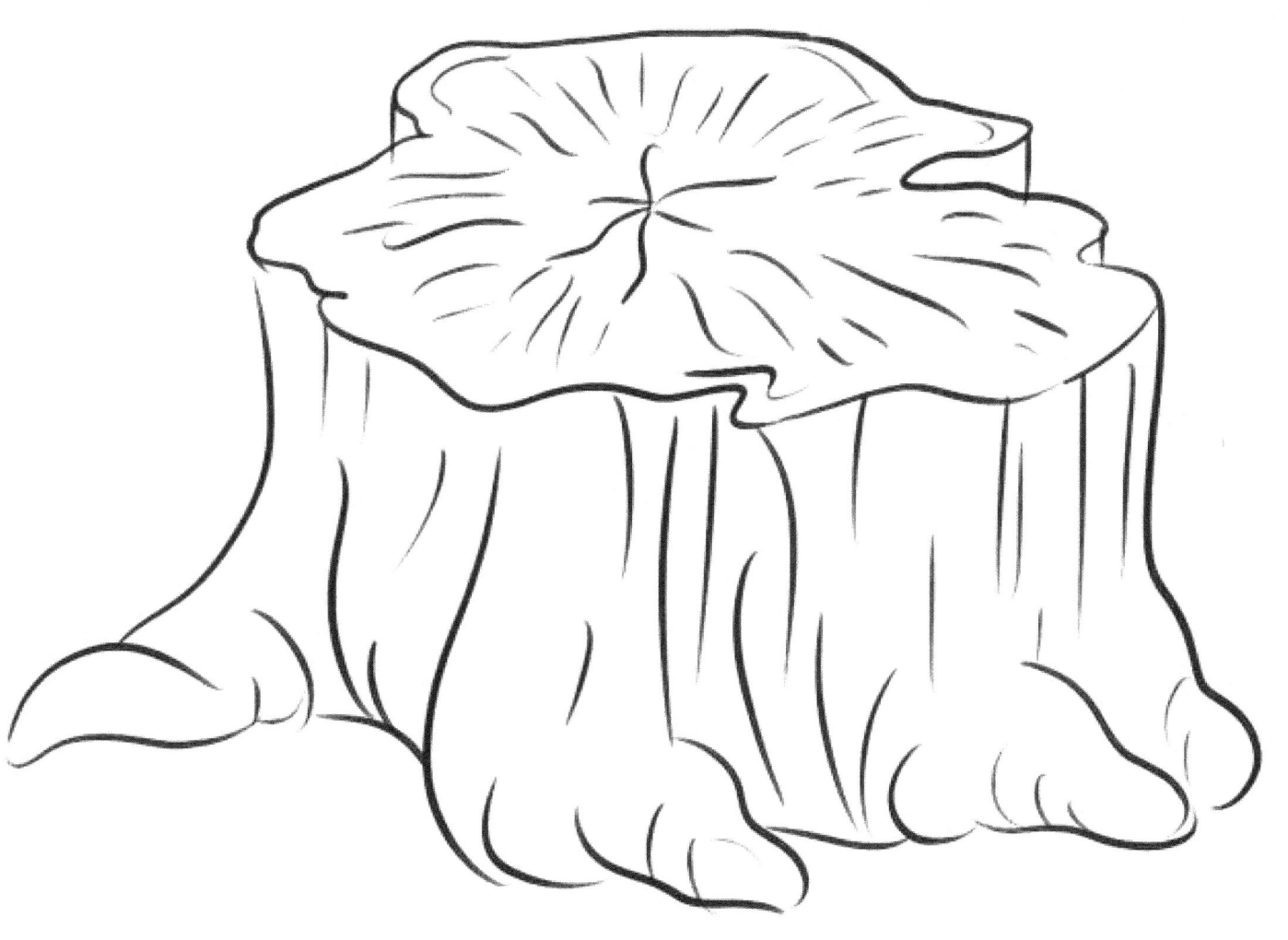

Tree stump